The Police Assessment Center: Important Keys for Success

The Police Assessment Center: Important Keys for Success

What You Need to Know and May Not Have Been Told

BARRY T. MALKIN

iUniverse, Inc.
New York Bloomington

The Police Assessment Center: Important Keys for Success
What You Need to Know and May Not Have Been Told

Copyright © 2009 Barry T. Malkin

All rights reserved. No part of this book may be used or reproduced by
any means, graphic, electronic, or mechanical, including photocopying,
recording, taping or by any information storage retrieval system
without the written permission of the publisher except in the case
of brief quotations embodied in critical articles and reviews.

iUniverse books may be ordered through booksellers or by contacting:

iUniverse
1663 Liberty Drive
Bloomington, IN 47403
www.iuniverse.com
1-800-Authors (1-800-288-4677)

Because of the dynamic nature of the Internet, any Web addresses or links
contained in this book may have changed since publication and may no longer be
valid. The views expressed in this work are solely those of the author and do not
necessarily reflect the views of the publisher, and the publisher hereby disclaims
any responsibility for them.

ISBN: 978-1-4401-6402-6 (sc)
ISBN: 978-1-4401-6404-0 (dj)
ISBN: 978-1-4401-6403-3 (ebk)

Printed in the United States of America

iUniverse rev. date: 12/16/2009

Acknowledgments

Joan Weiss, Sheila Beaman, Cathy Bolden, Josephine Perkins, Dr. Leisha Carter, Shireen Ambush, Katrina Barrett, Collin Corbin, Ronda LeBlanc, Trish Bittner

CONTENTS

1. About the Author 1

2. Why I Had to Write This Book........................3

3. The Assessment Center—Definition, Purpose and History 7

4. Training and Selection of the Assessors 25

5. Why the Extra Point Makes Such a Difference 35

6. Critical Concept Number One: Dimensions or Characteristics.......................................41

7. Critical Concept Number Two: Issues, Actions and Follow-Up Actions 47

8. The Relevance of Delegation..........................67

9. Simple Keys to Assessment Center Success 85

Chapter 1

ABOUT THE AUTHOR

I am a retired District of Columbia Metropolitan Police officer. I served on the force for thirty-three years and seven months. Of that time, I spent nine years in uniform patrol, eleven and a half as a uniform patrol sergeant, three years as a lieutenant both in patrol and as an equal employment opportunity specialist, eight years as a patrol captain and the final two and a half years at the Metropolitan Police Training Academy, first as the deputy director and later as acting director of the Testing and Standards Branch.

My other experience includes working briefly for the New Jersey Department of Personnel as a test development specialist for the rank of sergeant, as well as serving as an assessor in Arlington, Virginia, for the rank of lieutenant; in New Orleans, Louisiana, for the rank of lieutenant; in Tulsa, Oklahoma, for the rank of major; and in my department for the ranks of sergeant and detective grade one.

In 2001, I participated in the International Association of Chiefs of Police four-day Conference on Assessment Centers in St. Petersburg, Florida. In 2002, I personally conducted the training for outside-the-department lieutenants and captains who would later be the assessors for Washington, DC's Metropolitan Police Department's 2002 Promotional Process Assessment Center for sergeant, lieutenant and captain.

In 2003 and 2004, I was assigned the responsibility of creating my department's very first centralized Master Patrol Officer Selection Process. This included preparing the written and oral exercise scenarios, the assessor and item-writer training and the candidate orientation. I completed the process in May 2004. On Thursday, June 23, 2004, I turned in my gun and badge. On Friday, my last day at work, I arrived at the usual 0630 hours, and stayed a bit later than 1500, saying goodbye to and thanking my co-workers at the Training Academy.

The very next morning, Saturday, I signed the papers for my childhood dream, a bay-front condominium in Ocean City, Maryland. Captain Willie Smith, a co-worker friend of mine and a tremendous help to me during the 2002 promotional process, and Sheila Beaman, my invaluable management analyst who always had my back, had driven up to be with me. My wonderful girlfriend, Paula, was there too. I was now retired, and there would never be any more check-in or check-out times at cheap motels. How lucky was I!

Chapter 2

WHY I HAD TO WRITE THIS BOOK

Law enforcement is a truly wonderful career. I got into it on a fluke, and may or may not go into that in another book. However, I loved being a police officer most of the time, though there were times that were difficult, trying and so depressing that I came pretty close to getting out of Dodge. For the most part, though, police officers are able to experience life in a way that most people would never be able to do, or even imagine.

I have always taken great pride in doing things that help people. My superiors saw me as being a little different—as more than a "lock 'em up" cop. I went further than was required of me and employed discretion when I could. I guess some liked that. Because of this, early in my career I had the wonderful fortune of acquiring **rabbis.** In law enforcement, "rabbi" is a term of endearment for someone who looks out for and guides you. This absolutely does not mean that person will cover up improprieties or misconduct. In my career, especially, this was not true. Like most officers, I did do some things wrong and on one occasion conducted myself in a way that was *perceived* by some as wrong. For these minor infractions and perceived misconduct, not only could my rabbis not help me, but different police officials initially told me to resign. My rabbis, however, were there on each occasion to take me aside and talk to me. These were true mentors and coaches, through critical times, simply trying to make me a better police officer.

Though I feel that the expression "to give something back" is mostly overused and insincerely meant, that's what I want to do. I wrote this book to help those police officers who really love the job and want to better the profession to get promoted.

Some of the concepts and methods discussed will be very controversial. Some may make little sense at all. I know that, because I have coached and mentored many past and present police officials. All objected to or at least questioned some of the fundamental suppositions and theories that I brought to the table.

I cannot promise you that reading this book will get you promoted. I can tell you that the vast majority of the officers who have attended my private coaching/teaching sessions have been promoted during the applicable promotional time span. I will promise you one thing, though. When I do present something that I know will make you shake your head sideways, not up and down, I will give you a detailed explanation. Then you are on your own.

Finally, in the course of personally conducting seventy-six assessment center process feedback/coaching/teaching sessions with candidates who competed in the 2002 promotional process for sergeant, lieutenant and captain, I adopted the training style you will find in this book. It may at times be unfriendly, tough and most assuredly not politically correct. Though this doesn't reflect my true personality, my style will be that way at times to stress a point It will be that way because the method works. If you follow most of what I say, you will greatly improve your chances of doing well and might even blow your assessors away come assessment time. Good luck!

Chapter 3

THE ASSESSMENT CENTER—DEFINITION, PURPOSE AND HISTORY

An assessment center is a place where you are judged by a group or groups of individuals called **assessors**, who rate how well you would perform the position you are competing for. The exercises through which you demonstrate your **knowledge, skills and abilities**—usually referred to as **KSA's**—may include role-playing, oral and/or written responses to oral and/or written questions, panel interviews, question-and-answer sessions, brainstorming sessions, leadership sessions and more. Though all of the above exercises can be conducted at an assessment center, an assessment usually consists of one or two practical activities and written/administrative exercises.

The assessment is intended to have you demonstrate practical knowledge and skills, but it is just one part of the **promotional**

process, which also usually includes a separate question-and-answer booklet or written examination. For example, in almost all state and large municipal departments, the promotional process for corporals, sergeants, lieutenants and sometimes many higher ranks includes some type of competition among candidates. This competition will usually require each candidate to take a written examination, then shortly afterwards compete in an oral and/or written practical or field exercise. (For the remainder of this book, the term **field exercise** will refer to any assessment center testing exercise other than written/computer or administrative testing.) After being graded or scored on both the written test and the field exercise or exercises, the candidate will receive a final overall score that incorporates the weighting of each exercise.

Weighting simply means the mathematical importance your particular police department gives each exercise. For example, let's say both the written test and the assessment center exercise are worth 50 percent. There is a field of ten candidates. The best candidate gets 47 points on the written test and 40 points on the field exercise. The worst candidate gets 30 points on the written test and 20 points on the field exercise. In most departments, the candidates will then be placed on a promotional register in descending order, from the candidate who scored 87 to the candidate who scored 50. Then, let's say there are three position vacancies. Again usually, but not always, the candidates who had the top three scores will be promoted first.

The Police Assessment Center: Important Keys for Success

Though it is of no conceptual importance to this book, I want to mention something briefly. A few departments promote from a promotional register using a process called the banding method. This gives the chiefs of police and the higher-ups they answer to more leeway in the promotional process. For example, let's say a particular department's band is five. That means that any of the candidates who scored in the top five can be promoted. If there are three vacancies, the chief of police, if he or she wishes, can promote the candidates who scored third, fourth and fifth, completely passing over the candidates who scored first and second. There are also a few departments in which the chief can promote anyone on the register at his or her discretion, no matter that candidate's relative position. My opinion is that both of these methods are extremely unfair, with the latter being more blatantly unfair than the other. At the very least, the practices encourage cronyism.

The way that candidates are scored or graded varies greatly among and sometimes even within departments. In general, though, a **team of assessors**, usually only two or three, will score your performance on one or more exercises. The same assessors might score every exercise, or there may be completely different assessors scoring you for each exercise.

When you complete each exercise, the assessors will score you on many different criteria. Most departments require that the assessors come to an agreement about how well you performed, referred to as a **consensus**. For example, if you have two assessors, and one assessor scores you a 4 and the other assessor a 3 on one characteristic, on a scale of 1 to 10, they reach a consensus and give you a 3, 3.5, 4, or even a 10 for the exercise. (Don't worry about characteristics/dimensions and consensus now; I will go into detail later in the book.)

I will not attempt to get into the content or construct validity of these promotional processes; I'll leave that to greater scholars than me. Suffice it to say that if a precise benchmark study were done comparing the tens of thousands of police departments in this country, it would find that very few conduct their processes exactly alike. For instance, for promotion to sergeant, one department may weight the written exam as being worth 70 percent and the field exercise 30 percent. For promotion to lieutenant, that same department could weight the written exam at 40 percent and the field exercise 60 percent. The rationale might be that knowledge of the state or municipal code of laws and public safety and traffic regulations is much more important at the rank of sergeant—who is a trainer and on-site supervisor—than at the rank of lieutenant. Conversely, lieutenants need to know how to handle practical field situations as on-site commanders and managers, and if they don't know a particular law or regulation, they can always look it up in the office or ask a sergeant, corporal or master patrol officer on the scene.

There are many different opinions on assessment centers. I have never seen two police departments with even nearly identical processes. However, I will say that of the many dozens of processes that I have

The Police Assessment Center: Important Keys for Success

either studied or participated in, most were fair and competently measured a candidate's suitability for promotion.

This section of the chapter will be the most boring for most of you. It definitely is for me to write. It is important though, so I ask that you plod through it, maybe taking more than one sitting to do so. Why? It provides the basis for why I'm going to tell you many of the crazy and not-so-crazy things that I want you to do.

Assessment centers have been used in private industry in this country since the early 1900s. They have not, however, been used in police departments until relatively recently, the mid- to late-1970s. Here's why.

Since before the turn of the century, police departments throughout the United States largely relied on a paper examination as the main instrument for determining whether a candidate would be promoted. This examination would contain one or more type of question: true/false, multiple choice or essay.

While many departments used the written test exclusively, many also added a **suitability-** or **potential-for-promotion rating** to the mix. This rating was generally given to the candidate by his or her immediate supervisor in conjunction with approval by other members of the chain of command. Depending on the mathematical weighting (relative importance), the two scores would be compiled statistically, and the candidate would receive a final score or rating. A register would then be compiled that listed the candidate with the highest score at the top and the candidate with the lowest at the bottom. As vacancies for positions or grades became available, the candidates would be promoted from the list in the exact order that they were ranked. So, for example, let's say a department had five vacancies for sergeant. There were twenty candidates, who were ranked from 1 to 20, with 1 being the highest. Only those candidates numbered 1 through 5 would be promoted.

The serious flaw with this promotional process was with the suitability-for-promotion rating. First of all, the rating could be given arbitrarily and subjectively. In most departments, the rating did not require any written justification. Second, especially in small departments, it was at the very least rumored that the top ratings were given to only the "good old boys." Third, the suitability ratings in most departments were assigned after the written examination results were posted or announced. Thus, if a candidate scored highly on the written test, and for whatever reason the candidate's supervisors did not want him promoted, all they had to do to knock him to the bottom of the list was to give that candidate a low suitability rating.

Conversely, if a candidate did not do well on the written exam, a high suitability rating for a good old boy would at least put the candidate

The Police Assessment Center: Important Keys for Success

in contention, if not at or near the top of the list. This is not to say that a candidate's poor performance on a written test automatically meant he didn't deserve a high suitability rating. The same applies conversely: just because a candidate did well on a written exam does not mean that he or she should get a high suitability rating from supervisors. It's just that in biased hands, the suitability rating was an effective way to manipulate the promotional register.

In the mid-1970s, many of the larger police departments—especially the rank-and-file officers within those departments, generally privates, corporals, detectives and first-line supervisors—chose to have unions or bargaining agents represent them, especially for pay negotiations. The main reason was that rank-and-file officers (and occasionally low-, middle- and upper-level managers) had tried for years to negotiate pay raises so that their salaries, which were notoriously low for the risks they faced every day, were at least commensurate to those of other public servants and government workers. In most cases, city, state and county police departments had virtually no problems in hiring qualified candidates; therefore also in most cases, the political leaders of these jurisdictions, to save money, chose not to raise the salaries significantly.

The heads or police chiefs of their departments hardly ever came out publicly in favor of raises, either. Why should they? There was nothing in it for them. Not only that, it was a lose-lose situation. All police chiefs were, and still are, political appointees. Why would a police chief, especially one without the time or tenure to be able to retire, risk losing a well-paying and prestigious job, as well as a future pension, to publicly support a cause that wasn't going to happen? I definitely would not have, and I personally don't know of any police chiefs who did.

There were, of course, other issues the unions or bargaining agents brought to the negotiating table. Tours of duty, seniority and performance regarding assignments and days off, working conditions, outside employment and many other on- and off-duty matters became increasing concerns. Even though the missions of every department are technically worded differently, they are all basically the same. Every mission involves or should involve arresting criminals, preventing criminal acts and civil violations and reducing the public's fear of crime. Similarly, when it came to the working and pay issues that almost all departments wanted negotiated and improved, most issues were basically the same from department to department. Most officers wanted better working conditions, more leniency and flexibility in performing off-duty employment, fairer ways of designating assignments and assigning days off—and, of course, the elimination of the good-old-boy system in the promotional process.

Pressure on municipal leaders and police chiefs from the police unions and bargaining agents increased. Threats of sick-outs and work slowdowns also increased. Some actually occurred, though most were never publicly announced or admitted to. Finally, most departments reached acceptable compromises on most issues with the unions and the upper political and police echelon. One of the most significant compromises and successes was the partial collapse, but not the elimination of, the good-old-boy system inherent in the promotional process.

The first step to at least limit the effects of the old-boy system involved the suitability- or potential-for-promotion rating; it either had to be eliminated or its relative weight in determining the candidate's overall score had to be reduced. Most bargaining agents and union leaders enthusiastically welcomed this concept. Their members (again usually made up of only the rank and file, privates, corporals and possibly some supervisors—generally no managers) welcomed almost any change. They were rebellious and tired of being overlooked for candidates less qualified but in higher favor with the people in power. Most jurisdictional leaders (mayors, city managers, etc.) as well as their upper-level police department heads were very much opposed to any changes at all. They strongly resisted any reduction of their ability to both promote who they wanted and then to put their people in key positions.

Many departments simply got rid of the suitability rating. They realized that it had been grossly misused and abused in the past, and that its total elimination would spare them any controversy or litigation. Other departments kept the rating as part of their promotional process but reduced its overall weight in computing the candidate's final score. To take the place of the suitability rating, most departments implemented an assessment center process.

The assessors in these early assessment centers were usually high-ranking police officials from within their respective departments. The assessor panels normally were made up of either two or three members. Candidates had no input into the panels' membership. Some departments, though, allowed the candidates to know the members' names ahead of time and, if they desired, to eliminate one member from the list, to be replaced by another member, not of the candidate's choice. For instance, a candidate might choose to remove an official with whom she had a negative contact or an adverse experience.

Initially, the rank and file of most departments perceived both the addition of the assessment center as well as the elimination or reduction in importance of the suitability rating as improvements. However, there were still at least perceived problems. Candidates complained that allowing them to remove one assessor did not eliminate the possibility that the replacement assessor would be equally or even more biased. They also complained that whoever the assessors were, they brought inherent departmental favoritism to the table and that the process was still not a fair one.

Bargaining agents and union representatives met again with departmental and city and municipality leaders. Consulting firms and other think groups got involved in the processes. As a result, many departments decided to change the physical make-up of the assessor panel. Instead of being comprised of two or three high-ranking police officials from the department, one of the officials would be replaced by a psychologist or a human resources expert. This civilian member would have the same say as the other police members of the assessor panel in the candidates' final rating. It was perceived that adding a civilian professional with expertise in human relations and testing procedures would not only add to the reliability of the panels' evaluations but counteract any bias or favoritism the other police officials might harbor for the candidate.

As it turned out, many departments were initially very dissatisfied with the addition of a civilian member. There usually seemed to be a much greater disparity in scores given to candidates between the civilian members and the sworn than between the sworn themselves. While of course the two or three sworn members rarely scored each aspect of a candidate's performance exactly the same—nor should they—they usually came within one or two points of each other. However, scoring discrepancies were much wider when there was a civilian member on the assessment team. While it is true that in most assessment center scoring the assessors had to come to a consensus score for each dimension for each candidate, some assessment centers did not score that way. Some simply averaged the two or three assessors' scores, and that average became the candidate's final score.

It was not that the psychologists or human resources people weren't qualified to be assessors of a police candidate's behavior, knowledge, skills or abilities, it's just that they often either *brought* something extra or *lacked* something extra at the table. Sometimes they looked at these characteristics in a very different way than did the trained police assessors. While we could debate who the better assessors were, it would be impossible to prove one way or another statistically. For this book's purpose, it is not important at all. What is important, though, is that most departments soon eliminated civilian assessors as part of their assessment panels.

There were more conferences and workshops on the assessment center process. Police officials and test development specialists soon came to a pretty unanimously held but financially unpopular opinion: the most objective panel of assessors would consist of trained police assessors who had never seen or heard of the candidates being assessed. These would naturally be police officials from other police departments. They could not be from neighboring departments, to eliminate the chance that the candidates' and assessors' paths had crossed in the past. Therefore, the assessors would have to be from fairly distant departments.

Financially, this was an issue. The police assessors would have to be flown in and out of the jurisdiction or at the very least compensated for ground travel. They would have to be put up in a nice hotel. They would have to be fed at least two meals a day. Depending on their length of stay, they would have to be shown some amenities or taken to some enjoyable police or non-police related activities of interest.

Why all of these perks? If you did not provide them, not only would the police officials not want to ever return to the jurisdiction to be assessors, word would spread, sometimes like wildfire all over the country, to stay away from this inhospitable jurisdiction.

And that is where we are now. Most state, county and large city police departments have either adjusted or increased their budgets to accommodate outside police agencies that provide assessors. For those parts of the assessment process that are hand-written or typed, and for which the candidate does not have to appear before an assessment panel, things can be done a little differently to save time and money. Police assessors can be obtained from local or nearby jurisdictions, thus reducing the budget for travel expenses, room and meal accommodations. To ensure strict anonymity for the candidates, there must be no identifying names on the written or typed responses. This can be done easily enough by simply assigning each candidate a corresponding number, word or symbol.

Finally, as I close out this section of the chapter, I will mention that in their attempt to ensure more fairness and objectivity and to reduce candidate bias, a few departments have their candidates record their responses to the oral part of the assessment center exercise. This recording is done on cassette or DVD. This practice may or may not increase in popularity, as it too is not perfect. Cassettes and DVD's can be damaged or recorded incorrectly. They can also get lost or misplaced. I know personally of a situation in which cassettes were used, duplicates were made and stored at a different location than the originals, and one particular candidate's both original and duplicate disappeared.

Another barrier to objectivity—and though it's politically incorrect to discuss this—is the fact that the assessors can always tell the gender of the candidate, a vast majority of the time they can tell the race of the candidate, and sometimes they can even tell the ethnicity of the candidate.

So, as you see, the working of the assessment center is a continually evolving process with plenty of room to tweak the imperfections. You notice I said "tweak," for the process can never be perfect.

☆ ☆ ☆

As a rule of thumb, in order to beat any potential court challenge, the police assessors on any given panel must be or must have once been at least the rank of the candidates they will be assessing. That does not mean they must have had the same job description or done the same things, but simply that they have worked at the same rank or title.

For example, let's say candidates are competing for the rank of sergeant in Cookie County, Maryland. One of the main jobs as a

The Police Assessment Center: Important Keys for Success

sergeant in Cookie County is being a watch commander for a particular shift. Cookie County is using assessors from all over the country, all of whom are the rank of sergeant. It just so happens that most of these sergeant assessors have never been watch commanders in their respective departments because, in their departments, lieutenants perform that job. Despite this, they still have the task of assessing those candidates competing for the rank of sergeant, even though the assessors have never performed one of the tasks required for this particular position, that of watch commander.

Those of you competing for promotion for the first time may view this as totally unfair. You are right. That's the way it goes, though. Although it won't make you any happier, let me briefly tell you why. Most police departments take their promotional process seriously, *but not that seriously*. Most departments try to budget the bare minimum for a promotional process. Most departments experience trouble, ranging from minor difficulty to the equivalent of pulling teeth, in simply getting officials from other departments to serve as assessors. This is especially true when their services are required for several weeks. It's hard to imagine the staff and man hours required to do a thorough job analysis of every rank of every outside department that sends assessors to make sure that the job descriptions of these assessors are the same as or similar to the job descriptions of the ranks that the candidates are competing for.

To confound things even further, nowadays it's almost fashionable for some departments to periodically change the job descriptions for the various ranks. For example, in one major, big city department, the job of patrol watch commander was reassigned within six months after a new chief of police was appointed. Where previously there had been sergeant watch commanders on midnights and lieutenant watch commanders on days and evenings, suddenly there were only lieutenant watch commanders on all shifts. Several new chiefs and about seven years later, captains were mandatory watch commanders on day and evening shifts, and lieutenants could command the watch only on midnights. About a year later, that same chief changed things again, to captains only, no exceptions. Unauthorized deviations from this policy resulted in the disciplining of district commanders.

Suffice it to say, you need to know that the assessors rating you may have different job descriptions than the position you are competing for. Remember this as we continue our discussion.

The Police Assessment Center: Important Keys for Success

Important Points to Remember

- The police assessment center is a practical exercise.
- The weight or importance it is assigned in determining your promotional status varies greatly among police departments across the country.
- It is here to stay.
- Your assessors will be intelligent police officials.
- They will probably have never seen or heard anything about you.
- They will have little if any bias for or against you.

Chapter 4

TRAINING AND SELECTION OF THE ASSESSORS

At this point, it's probably unclear to most of you how this book gives you an extra edge over your competition. Some of you may have an idea of the reason for my slightly long-winded introduction. Hopefully, this chapter will begin to guide you to where you would like to be.

Although most departments' orientation and training sessions are run differently, most have certain elements in common. First, the police officials from the outside departments assemble. It may be in a classroom, a hotel room, an auditorium, etc. At least one member of the testing/assessment center unit is present to welcome the assessors. There may be one or more high-ranking officials present from the hosting department.

There are two major schools of thought as to whether ranking officials from the hosting department should welcome all the assessors and spend some time speaking to the outside assessors. Interestingly, the schools of thought are about as far apart as possible.

The first school of thought is that the initial presence of a chief of police or other high-ranking police official to welcome and talk to the assessors signals that the assessment center is of critical importance to the hosting department. It shows that the hosting department takes this process extremely seriously. This is important for the following reasons, which aren't often admitted.

First, most departments have some difficulty getting volunteers to come to their jurisdiction for an extended period. For a myriad of family-related and other personal reasons, most police officials do not want to travel to other states to put in long days of intensive paperwork and evaluations. Therefore, outside departments more often than not *draft* their officials to travel and be assessors. So you see that from the very start, the hosting department may be receiving some reluctant assessors.

Second, the departments that cannot get volunteers and thus send reluctant draftees will not send their very best officials. They do not want to anger their outstanding officials, who they may have a critical need for at home. Losing them for several weeks of assessment may have a negative impact on operations in their home department. While police departments normally do not send their worst officials or ones who might embarrass their department, they usually send those officials who are marginal or at best average in ability and qualifications.

Third, unless the jurisdictions the assessors are going to are especially desirable—for reasons like great climate, great nightlife or a reputation for short work days—the only volunteers will normally be trying to get away from something or someone for a short period of time. They may be trying to escape a spouse or bad relationship, a bad boss at work, an unpleasant assignment or detail or the like.

When all of these things are considered, it's clear that at least some, if not a majority, of the outside assessors may be less than desirable not only in their knowledge, skills and abilities, but also in motivation and sense of purpose. It is specifically because of this that the highest-ranking member of the hosting department, or his or her designee, should be there to welcome the assessors and talk with them about the assessment process individually and/or as a group. This lets the assessors know that the chief or designee of the hosting department knows about them and knows intimately about the assessment process. At the very least, it gives the assessors a sense of purpose and tends to motivate all but the most unmotivated.

There is, however, a second school of thought: there should be no sworn members at all to welcome and explain the process to the assessors. This school suggests that the presence of any sworn, high-ranking members of the hosting department could unfairly bias or prejudice the outside assessors. Those who subscribe to this thinking sometimes go as far as prohibiting the assessors from having any contact with any sworn members of the department during their non-working time or days off in the hosting jurisdiction. Only civilian members of the hosting department, civilians from the city or state government or civilians whom the department contracted to conduct the assessment center can have any contact with the assessors.

Now we get to the actual training. After the initial welcoming, whether by sworn officials or civilians, there is an orientation of some type. The assessors are given a brief history and overview of the department and of the jurisdiction it serves. They usually receive map of the jurisdiction and a breakdown of how police service is performed in the precincts, districts, patrol service areas, etc. They are told about the rank structure and the duties and responsibilities of each rank. Additional emphasis is usually placed on the rank the assessors will be assessing. This orientation process may take from one to several hours, depending on how many questions the assessors ask.

Next, the assessors are usually, but not always, given an overview of the hosting department's assessment process. The overview may be just a brief description of the **phase** (portion of testing) that they are assessing and the rating process/rating scale they will use, or it may include a detailed analysis of all of the phases in the assessment center,

The Police Assessment Center: Important Keys for Success

including the actual test development, justification for rating scales employed, validity and reliability studies, etc.

After the orientation is completed, the actual training begins. Trainers have prepared sample scenarios in advance, which may be written on paper and handed out to the assessors. Alternately, they may be written but not distributed to the assessors, but instead read aloud by the trainer.

At the same time, the assessors are given a cheat sheet that contains all of the responses that an ideal candidate for the rank tested would give for that particular scenario. These responses are listed in bullets (little circles or squares) that the assessors can check off as being the candidate's response. These responses have been prepared for the training session by the hosting department's testing staff and have been independently reviewed and probably re-reviewed by other testing staff members or other supervisory and management personnel.

The sample scenario could involve a myriad of things. It could be a crime problem, a personnel issue, a nuisance issue, a domestic dispute, a traffic control situation or combinations of the aforementioned. The assessors are then presented with actors who play the part of the candidates. These actors may be civilian employees or police officials who have been guided in advance as to how to answer or respond to the scenarios. Usually there will be only two or three actors at a time for these particular training scenarios.

After each actor candidate makes a presentation, the assessors are asked to evaluate each actor's performance. Using cheat sheets or response guides as guidelines, each assessor rates each actor. They do so by simply checking off the bullets next to each correct response listed on their sheets. If the candidate says something that is not listed on their sheet, they simply handwrite the response onto the sheet. Using the sample scoring sheets that they have marked on, they rate each actor's responses by category. See the following hypothetical example:

Assessor 1 rating Candidate 1 for Sergeant

Job Knowledge   2

Personal Relations   3

Problem-Solving   5

Oral Expression   3

Judgment   3

Assessor 2 rating Candidate 1 for Sergeant

Job Knowledge   3

Personal Relations   2

Problem-Solving   3

Oral Expression   5

Judgment   4

The Police Assessment Center: Important Keys for Success

Let's say that these are the scores for Candidate 1, using a five-point scale. As you can see, Assessors 1 and 2 rated the candidate differently. Not only is this not unusual, it is the norm. Assessors 1 and 2 will then privately discuss with each other why they rated Candidate 1 the way they did. Then they will come to what I mentioned earlier in the book as **consensus.**

Here is an example of this consensus:

Candidate #1 Final Rating after Consensus

Job Knowledge	4
Personal Relations	2
Problem-Solving	2
Oral Expression	4
Judgment	3

Now let's examine how the assessors may have arrived at the ratings for this candidate. When the assessors got together in private, they realized that they had slightly different ideas about what candidate displayed in the areas of problem-solving and job knowledge. After further discussion and comparing notes, which revealed that many of the positive responses they checked off related to job knowledge, they decided that the candidate had a lot of job knowledge. Thus, while initially they gave the candidate a 2 and 3 respectively in the area of job knowledge, the candidate received a final rating of 4.

Both assessors also agreed that their respective ratings of 5 and 3 for problem-solving were inaccurate; many of the candidate's positive responses actually related more to job knowledge. They agreed together that the candidate demonstrated very little problem-solving and dropped the candidate's score to a 2.

For the personal relations dimension, they agreed that a 3 rating was too high and dropped the candidate to a 2.

As far as oral expression was concerned, Assessor 1 admitted feeling that the candidate expressed herself well but was almost timid and at times could not be heard. Assessor 2 agreed but thought that the candidate's clarity and choice of words in expressing herself were excellent. After just a brief discussion, they came to a consensus and a rating of 4.

The two assessors had a difficult time agreeing on the candidate's judgment. They had both checked off just about the same bullets related to judgment. They are taught in this assessor training to specifically avoid what is called the **halo effect**. This simply means the candidate's performance in certain categories, whether good or bad, should not influence the evaluation in others. Simply, each category should be evaluated on its own merits. As normal human beings, though, the assessors will be subject to a certain amount of subjectivity. Don't let anyone ever tell you that the assessors can totally avoid this halo effect.

The Police Assessment Center: Important Keys for Success

In this case, Assessor 2 went along with Assessor 1 and came to a consensus score of 3. Assessor 2 might never admit it publicly, but since the candidate had scored so low in personal relations and problem-solving, he went along with Assessor 1's rating and agreed to lowering the score to 3.

To wrap up this very simple but realistic hypothetical evaluation, the candidate was given 16 points by Assessor 1 and 17 points by Assessor 2. The candidate's final score, though, was 15 points.

Each assessment team of two or three is given this same scenario and discusses their final evaluations with the trainer. The trainer may then give several more practice scenarios to the assessment teams until the trainer feels the teams are ready to receive and rate the actual candidates for promotion. When both the assessment teams and the trainer feel comfortable, the assessment process can begin.

Important Points to Remember

- Except in rare circumstances, your assessors will be from police departments other than your own.

- There will always be assessors who not only did not want to leave their department to come to your jurisdiction, but also did not want to be assessors. However, such assessors will usually be in the minority.

- Though your assessors will generally be of a higher rank than you, they may not have performed the particular job skill that the rank you are competing for involves.

- Assessors will usually not be the very best or very worst from their respective departments. They will usually be about average, and some may be marginal.

- Assessors know very little, if anything, about your department.

- Their training and orientation period is brief at best.

- There are some exceptions, but usually you will be assessed by two or three assessors. (I've known some departments to have as many as five per candidate.)

- You will be rated on a point scale by each individual assessor.

- The assessors will then agree on just one score for each characteristic or dimension. This is called a consensus. (Some departments use averaging to get the final score. These, however, are the exception.)

Chapter 5

WHY THE EXTRA POINT MAKES SUCH A DIFFERENCE

If the example in the previous chapter had been a real case, the fact that the candidate for sergeant received the score of 3 in the judgment dimension could be catastrophic to her hopes of promotion. Had she received a 4, her final score would have been 16, rather than 15. The difference of just one point can have a tremendous impact on any candidate, depending on a myriad of factors, such as the number of vacancies, the number of candidates, the weighting of the assessment phase of the promotional process, and so forth.

That one-point difference could prevent the candidate from getting promoted to sergeant. Just for example, let's say there were twenty-five vacancies for sergeant, and fifty candidates competed in the promotional process. With a score of 15, the previous candidate ended up number thirty on the promotional list. She did not get promoted.

Had she scored that extra one point and received a final score of 16, in our example she would have ended up twentieth on the promotional register and been promoted to the rank of sergeant. That one extra point not given to her by her assessment team—maybe because she was a little timid, maybe because she was a little weak on problem-solving, maybe because she lacked a bit in human relations—caused her to not get promoted.

Our hypothetical candidate was very disheartened. She loved being a police officer, was very bright, and obviously had a lot of good job knowledge. Before she joined the department, she had served a tour of duty in the United States Army as a commissioned officer. She was a natural leader. She had worked for many years on the street and probably knew how to solve problems, probably was very assertive on the street, and probably had very good personal relations with her peers, supervisors and the community. She simply did not display those characteristics well at test time.

When she found out that both assessors had initially given her higher scores than the final one she received after they came to consensus, she became upset. As previously described, one assessor initially gave her 17 points and the other 16. She could not understand how her final score could have been 15.

The Police Assessment Center: Important Keys for Success

She found out the above information by requesting a feedback session. Most departments allow the candidates to receive a copy of, or at least view, the actual sheets of paper that the assessors use to score the candidates' performance. This means that the candidates can see their scores for each dimension, along with any additional written comments about their strengths or weaknesses. In these written comments she read that after discussion, both assessors felt that they rated her higher than they should have in the judgment category. Hence they lowered their consensus score to 15, which they had every right to do.

Our candidate initially was very bitter. She felt that not only did she do better than she was scored, but also that the assessment process was unfair and flawed. She was so disappointed, in fact, that she never took part in the promotional process again. She was not only disgusted with the process, she was angry at the department for subscribing to the process. She eventually got a good inside job off the street, at which she excelled. She also stayed on the department way past the minimum optional retirement but eventually retired with an annuity of about $50,000 a year.

Had she gotten promoted to sergeant and had she remained on the department the same amount of time, her retirement annuity would have been about $58,000 per year. That assumes that she remained at the rank of sergeant. In the event that she had attained a higher rank, her retirement annuity could have been much larger, depending, of course, on the rank she had attained.

Let's say this officer went through the promotional process with roughly five years on the job. She retired after her thirtieth year. There was a difference of about $4,000 per year between an officer's and a sergeant's salary. Very roughly speaking, that amounts to about $100,000 over the course of her career. This is a significant amount, especially when added to the $8,000 difference in annuity money for the remainder of her life.

So what's the point? Money is far from everything, but it is important. Don't believe for one second that it is not one of the primary motivating factors for most professions, including law enforcement. I know that some studies and surveys rank salary or earning potential very low as motivational factors in law enforcement careers, but don't believe them. They are either flawed, their questions are skewed or their samples are preselected or nonrepresentative of the average street officer. Based on my experience, the truth is that job security and salary (which includes health and retirement benefits) are the number one and two most important motivational factors for most law enforcement personnel. The truth also is that a significant minority of officers would reverse the ranking, placing salary at the top.

For our hypothetical Candidate 1, who eventually had a wonderful and rewarding career, one single point—just one—could have made a significant, if not drastic, difference in her lifestyle. It could have affected her decisions about renting rather than buying a home, or about how many children she could afford to raise, and so many other smaller lifestyle

The Police Assessment Center: Important Keys for Success

issues. That one point probably made a big difference in her quality of life. That's not at all to say she did not have a wonderful quality of life, but just maybe it could have been much better. That is the point.

The remaining chapters will be devoted to helping you get an extra point or maybe two, nothing more. This is not an assessment center course, nor will it prepare you for your experience at an assessment center. I strongly recommend—especially for officers who have never competed for promotion using an assessment center—that candidates participate in practice assessment centers conducted by other active or retired members of their department, or by private consultants or companies. Whether or not they're the best, it will help to go through the process, thereby eliminating some of the nervousness and fear of the unknown that most candidates experience.

So study hard. Know your laws of arrest, search and seizure, and the criminal code in your jurisdiction. Learn and know your traffic and municipal regulations. Know the organizational chart of your department and the chain of command within every department. You must have solid knowledge of all of these things. As soon as you feel that you do, read on. We're going to have some fun with the system and kick some butt in the assessment center process!

Important Points to Remember

- A difference of just one numerical point in your assessment can determine whether you receive the promotion you seek.

- This is true because that one point could make a huge difference in your ranking on your promotional list or register. In my department I've seen one point make the difference of from ten to twenty positions. (Of course there may be other factors that contribute to your numerical ranking and the one or fraction point significance. These may include seniority, residential preference, education, etc.) These factors will vary from department to department.

- The most important things that matter to most police officers are job security and salary.

- Spend most of your time studying your department's required study materials on which your test and assessment center will be based.

- Only after thoroughly doing so can the following chapters sharpen and hone your skills, thus giving you a huge advantage toward promotion.

Chapter 6

CRITICAL CONCEPT NUMBER ONE: DIMENSIONS OR CHARACTERISTICS

The assessment center exercises, scenarios and problems are usually created by a preselected police official or group of officials from your department These police officials are generally at least one rank higher than the rank you are competing for. For example, if you are competing for the rank of sergeant, the police officials creating the scenarios will probably be the rank of lieutenant or higher. These police officials may be two or three ranks higher, but probably not more than two.

The theory behind this is really quite simple, though to my limited knowledge it has never been statistically supported or proven true. The theory is that, to construct valid scenarios for a particular rank, one must have served in that rank so successfully that he was able to demonstrate, in competition, the knowledge, skills and ability to be promoted to at least the next rank. Following from this theory, it is also commonly thought that those officials several ranks higher—for instance, commanders, deputy chiefs, etc.—have probably lost some of the street-level knowledge and skills necessary to the rank of sergeant. A newly promoted lieutenant, however, or a captain who moved up in the ranks pretty quickly from sergeant and then lieutenant, would probably have a better memory and recall of the "stuff" needed to create the exercises, problems and scenarios in a sergeant's assessment center.

What is this "stuff" that I'm talking about? It includes a lot of things. It includes situations that the scenario writers feel you must be able to handle at the rank of sergeant. It includes problems that their own sergeants currently have in properly supervising some street situations. It includes thorny personnel issues such as increased domestic violence in officers' families, personal indebtedness or increasing tardiness for duty assignments. It includes training in current critical areas of importance that a sergeant must be able to conduct. It includes all of the above and much more.

Now we begin discussing the first critical concept. When the police officials sit down to write the scenarios that you will be given to handle and solve, then judged and scored on, they do so with only three primary and ongoing thoughts in their minds:

The Police Assessment Center: Important Keys for Success

1. The situation must be valid and must apply at the rank you are competing for.

2. The situation must be able to be handled within whatever time parameters have been set up and previously announced to or published for the candidates.

3. Each situation must be constructed to elicit a fairly wide range of responses from the candidate. Why is this? Because in these responses candidates must be able to demonstrate their knowledge of the characteristics or dimensions on which they are being measured.

Somewhere in your department's assessment center formal announcement or maybe in an orientation session, you will be given a set of dimensions, or characteristics, upon which your assessors will rate you on a numerical scale. The rating scale will usually be a scale of 1 to 5, 1 to 7 or 1 to 9. These dimensions or characteristics will vary from department to department, and sometimes will vary within the same department over a period of time. That said, they usually involve some of the following:

1. Job Knowledge
2. Problem-Solving
3. Community Relations
4. Human or Personal Relations
5. Judgment

6. Written Expression

7. Oral Expression

Let's say that your assessment center exercise consists of ten problems or scenarios that you have to address. Those ten problems or scenarios have been prepared for you by police department experts in their fields, and usually in conjunction with, or at least reviewed by, test development specialists. This is to ensure that in order to address each scenario properly or solve each problem correctly, *candidates will have had to demonstrate the above dimensions.* This is one of the most, if not the most, important points I will stress in this book.

The police officials and test development specialists who prepare the scenarios for your assessment center usually spend a minimum of several months preparing them. Again, they prepare them in such a way that *in order to respond with the proper solutions*, you will *automatically*—probably even without your knowledge—*demonstrate most if not all of the above dimensions.*

As stated previously, these scenarios have been reviewed and probably re-reviewed more than once, and would not have been given to you if determining the correct responses to them did not force you to display most of the above dimensions. There would be no purpose for the scenarios if solutions to them did not incorporate the dimensions, including job knowledge, community relations, problem solving, etc.

The Police Assessment Center: Important Keys for Success

Having said all that, here is critical concept number one:

ON THE DAY OF THE ASSESSMENT, DO NOT, AND I EMPHASIZE DO NOT, THINK ABOUT THE DIMENSIONS ON WHICH YOU ARE GOING TO BE MEASURED.

There is enough stuff going on in your head that day. Most people will probably be very nervous and have some anxiety. This is a huge day for you. Very possibly your whole career depends on your performance this day. The people who prepared the assessment center have had months to worry about the dimensions. They have done their utmost to prepare scenarios that, *if you simply do the right things, will elicit these dimensions from you, without you even knowing it.*

The scenario writers have thought about the dimensions for months, and your dwelling on them or even thinking about them on this nerve-wracking day could destroy your chances for promotion. I personally have seen this happen more times than you might believe.

Important Points to Remember

- During your assessment center exercises, you will be required to demonstrate your proficiency of certain specific characteristics.

- These characteristics are more commonly referred to as dimensions.

- These exercises were created in such a way that by simply handling them properly and thoroughly, you will demonstrate your proficiency in these dimensions.

- You may not be able to demonstrate all of these dimensions in every exercise, but there will be enough exercises to enable you to demonstrate, many times over, all of the dimensions your assessors are looking for.

- If you have the time after you complete the paper or computer part of your assessment center exercises, you may go back and check to see if you have displayed as many dimensions as possible in each individual exercise. You probably will not have the time.

- Whatever you do, while you are handling each exercise, do not think individually about each dimension. You are facing something that may determine the most important part of your career path, and you must avoid as many distractions as possible.

Chapter 7

CRITICAL CONCEPT NUMBER TWO: ISSUES, ACTIONS AND FOLLOW-UP ACTIONS

The next critical concept *does* involve thinking about something constantly. Here is critical concept number two:

YOU MUST ALWAYS KEEP IN MIND THE FOLLOWING THREE THINGS, IN ORDER OF IMPORTANCE: ISSUES, ACTIONS AND FOLLOW-UP ACTIONS.

Because each aspect of this second critical concept is so important, I am going to discuss each of them individually.

ISSUES

For every scenario, you must identify the basic components or **issues** of the scenario. *Do not assume* that the assessors know that you know them. Even if you have to almost repeat certain things verbatim that are in the scenario in front of you, do so. This is not a waste of time; rather, it's a valuable use of your time. Here is why.

Let's say that, in your scenario, a man claiming to have a gun forces his way into his ex-wife's home and threatens to kill her unless she tells him where his baby is. Before the wife's 911 call is disconnected, she tells the dispatcher that she hid the baby in the house. When your officers arrive, there is no answer at the locked door.

First, let the assessors know that you know that you have a **hostage situation**. Then you should then tell them *why* this is a hostage situation. It will take you only approximately ten seconds to say the following:

1. Someone may be armed.
2. Someone is threatening someone's life.
3. Officer safety is at issue.
4. There is no answer at the door, and the door is locked.
5. A baby's safety is involved, and the baby's location is not known.

You have told the assessors the issues. This is very important!

Then let's assume that you screw up everything else in the scenario. The actions you take are wrong. The follow-up is wrong or nonexistent. By letting the assessors know that you at least recognized the situation for what it was, you will get some credit for two or more dimensions.

The Police Assessment Center: Important Keys for Success

First, you had the **job knowledge** to recognize that you had a hostage situation and why. Second, you showed good **judgment** in terms of concern for officer safety and recognizing that no answer at the door meant you should treat the event as a hostage situation.

So even if you do everything else wrong with the scenario, you literally get one or more points simply for identifying the issues. In this case scenario, in my opinion, job knowledge and judgment overlap. The assessors might think differently. They might, for instance, determine that the specific reasons why you declared this a hostage situation involved only the dimension of job knowledge. Maybe they gave you only a point for judgment and nothing for job knowledge. But my point is that you got a point for something, or perhaps even two points.

Assessors from other departments come from different mind-sets, experiences, job cultures, etc. What one assessor calls job knowledge, another calls judgment. But however you are rated, you are guaranteed to get something rather than nothing. The one or two points you receive for demonstrating knowledge of the issues may make the difference in getting that promotion. On my former department's promotional registers for sergeant, a single point could have been the difference of twenty, thirty or sometimes more slots. **Point taken?**

ACTIONS

For every scenario, you must take **actions**. The actions are what you do to address the scenario or solve the problem. These actions *must*, and I stress *must*, be as specific as possible. For example, in a hostage situation, you need to establish a **command post**. Telling your assessors that you are doing so is not enough. You need to tell them the following:

1. The reason a command post is necessary;
2. Where the command post is;
3. What the inner and outer perimeters are, as well as the kill-zone;
4. Exactly what equipment or resources you will obtain or have someone else obtain for the command post;
5. Who will be in charge at the command post;
6. Who you will get to staff the command post;
7. What notifications you will make regarding the establishment of the command post.

For example, look at number four above, equipment and resources. If you tell the assessors that you will need to provide additional lighting at the scene, you are not doing enough. You must tell the assessors exactly *whom you will contact* to get the lighting and *what equipment* will provide the light. For example, indicate that you will request the appropriate police official in the chain of command to notify the official in charge of the helicopter unit to provide aerial lighting for the scene. In this same way, you should notify the National Guard or state police to respond with trucks with high-intensity street lighting. You will need to identify any other agencies and the equipment or resources that they can provide. Of course, it's best to know who in the chain of command in your department actually has the authority to do these things, but *even if you do them yourself without knowing proper protocol,* the assessors will most likely give you some credit for your attention to detail and specific responses.

Make sure any necessary warnings are issued to the community. Be specific about what warnings are to be issued and by what means. For example, you might instruct the public information officer to notify local radio and television stations to alert the public about street closings around the incident area.

As a part of every command post there should be emergency medical staff. Know your department's protocol regarding who to have standing by in case of injuries to your officers or victims of the hostage scene. Though it's fairly obvious that some sort of emergency medical services unit or ambulance unit should be requested to respond to the scene, the assessors will be most impressed by the candidate who attempts to secure extra emergency services personnel on board an ambulance, along with several fire trucks staffed with extra emergency personnel. The candidate should tell the assessors why. The extra emergency services personnel are requested in case there are more victims and injuries than anticipated. In case ladder rescue or entry is necessary, and in the remote case of a deliberate or accidental fire, fire trucks are standing by. The candidate could also request that a physician from a local hospital or medical facility be transported to the scene to aid if immediate life-saving efforts are needed.

Establish specific entrance and exit routes. These are not only necessary for emergency services personnel, but for uninvolved community members who have to be allowed into and out of the critical incident. Even further, specific exit routes must be in place in case an evacuation is required.

It is of utmost importance that all the officers who are part of the command post are as comfortable as reasonably possible under the circumstances. As the circumstances allow in your particular scenario, try to ensure that there is some sort of commissary unit or at least a supply of cold water and hot coffee and tea. Make sure officers have access to portable toilets or other restroom facilities. Here again, your assessors will be impressed if you can tell them exactly whom you or your subordinate will contact, or whom you will recommend to your superior that he or she contact, to provide these services.

In our example, you tell the assessors that you will recommend to your lieutenant that the Mayor's Command Post be given a *request* from the Department of Public Works to provide portable toilets. Your will tell the assessors that you will notify the supervisor in charge of the division that oversees the commissary unit to *request* a commissary truck. If the situation has the potential to be prolonged, especially if there is inclement or severe weather, you would recommend to your lieutenant that the Special Operations Division be contacted with a *request* for a mobile command bus from which at least some of the staging operation for the hostage situation can be conducted.

Why the emphasis on "requesting"? Depending on the protocol in each department, only certain ranks can demand things. Some ranks can only request. Requesting should cover you, because it shows you know what you need even though you might not be in a position to get it.

The candidate who takes these extra steps is probably going to go way beyond what the average candidate will tell the assessors. All these steps may not be possible in your department or particular jurisdiction, but I give these examples to make you think out of the box. Many of you reading this may view some of these tactics as a bit unrealistic and unreasonable. They very well might be in your particular venue. My only point is to be **creative and proactive**. As long as your responses are logical and in the best interest of public safety, your assessors will probably recognize that they are used in their departments. If not, they will recognize that they *should* be part of their department's protocol.

The worst-case scenario is that you do not exactly follow the protocol of your department, or you overdo your response and you get no extra credit. Believe me, you will lose nothing. Instead, you will probably get some extra credit for functional creativity and critical thinking. And even though you may not receive this extra credit in actual points for that particular scenario, it will add to what I referred to earlier as the forbidden and demonized **halo effect**. When the assessors are forced to come to a consensus on your final score in a particular dimension such as judgment or problem-solving—and if the scores range between a 4 and a 5 or a 6 and a 7—guess what? You have a good chance of receiving the higher score. Not a sure thing, but a probable one.

FOLLOW-UP ACTIONS

Finally, you must have, for every scenario, something that is far too frequently left out: **follow-up actions**. I can't overemphasize the importance of these actions.

For *every* scenario or problem, there are follow-up actions that are important. At test time, the more follow-up actions that you take, the better your chances of doing well and getting that promotion. In real-life situations, you may not take all of the actions; that's OK. What's important is that taking these actions at test time will, it is hoped, translate into taking them in the field when you get promoted. You will at least think about them when you get in the field. You will think about them in roll call. You will think about them when doing investigations

The Police Assessment Center: Important Keys for Success

and writing reports or action plans. You will never forget assessment day, trust me. Hopefully your memories will be good ones.

Follow-up is probably the most underrated part of what you must do in your assessment center scenarios. It is also usually the candidates' worst-performed component. Why do candidates usually do so poorly on follow-up? The answer is very simple. It's because they perform this element the worst in real life, on their job. For various reasons that are not important for this book, cops are great at taking action on the issues, but once the situation is resolved, they usually do very minimal, if any, follow-up. I could easily write several long and complicated chapters on this component. The objective here, though, is to give you the basics of follow-up that are so often overlooked by your own assessors, supervisors and managers in the field in real time. Your assessors' cheat sheets, which we discussed earlier, will probably list many of these follow-up actions. If they don't, the assessors may not be looking for them. And if they are not looking for these follow-up actions, they will be *so impressed* when you give them, that you will get that extra point.

In your follow-up, you must always consider what to do regarding your **personnel** and what to do regarding your **actual crime scene scenario**.

Regarding personnel, for every scenario think **reward, punishment and training**. In our previous mini-scenario example, there is no conclusion. You are just recognizing the hostage situation for what it is and taking actions to resolve it successfully. The scenario did not mention any personnel actually completing work; therefore, there is no need to take any corrective action or to recommend disciplinary action for bad decisions or bad work by your personnel. However, if you do get a scenario that involves completed work or personnel taking action, and there is a need to reward, correct or discipline, *you must always do so.*

Good work can be rewarded verbally and informally, or documented in writing. Telling someone she did a good job and/or thanking her can go a long way. A written commendation makes this thank-you a permanent part of the officer's or supervisor's personnel record. Today, we as supervisors and managers must do things a lot differently than we did thirty or forty years ago. Without a long debate about whether things were better or worse a long time ago, the general rule today is to **always reward your personnel, at least verbally, for very good or above-average work, and to always document in writing, then at least counsel verbally, unsatisfactory or bad work.**

If you follow these guidelines, the worst possibility is that your assessors may feel you are overdoing things a bit in your handling of the scenarios. Even so, more importantly, you are demonstrating to them that you **recognize and take action** on both the positives and the negatives. That does not mean you have to punish or reprimand your personnel for unsatisfactory performance. It does mean, though, that

The Police Assessment Center: Important Keys for Success

when you do correct personnel, you should document it on paper so you have what I call a **temporary permanent file**.

As more and more departments use performance standards in assigning days off, shifts, assignments, etc. documentation is critical. It is especially so when you are challenged by unions or bargaining agents, or in any form of litigation. The reason I say "temporary" permanent file is that some departments allow for removal of this documentation after a period of time; others do not. The important thing is to do the documentation and make sure your assessors know exactly why and how you are rewarding and why and how you are documenting and correcting your personnel's performance. Be as specific as possible.

Since every department varies in the forms of praise/reward or corrective/disciplinary action that can be taken at specific ranks, know before assessment day what you are allowed to do administratively at the rank you are competing for. The assessors will reward you for demonstrating knowledge of the appropriate actions. By the same token, if during your assessment you overstate what you can actually do at the rank you are competing for, you might not get any rewards at all. We'll examine this in another sample scenario.

In this scenario, you are a newly promoted sergeant. One of your young and aggressive officers spots a vehicle he believes matches the lookout for one that was involved in a homicide a few days earlier. He attempts to stop the vehicle, but the driver refuses to pull over. A high-speed pursuit then ensues. As the fleeing vehicle runs a red light with the officer close behind, the officer does not slow down and T-bones another civilian vehicle that enters the intersection perpendicular to him. The officer and the driver of the other vehicle are seriously hurt. Other units involved in the pursuit eventually catch the suspected felon after he crashes into a retaining wall and overturns. The suspect eventually admits to the homicide and is successfully prosecuted and sentenced to many years in jail.

Now you have to look at what the officer did that was positive as well as what he did that was negative or negligent. You also look at what your department will allow *you personally* to do. As I said earlier, you must know your bounds in the area of reward and punishment; at different ranks you can do different things. If there are certain things you cannot do at your prospective rank, you still must know what you can **recommend** that other people in different positions should do.

In this scenario, the officer remembered the lookout given days earlier for an automobile involved in a homicide. He tried to initiate a felony stop. When that failed, he attempted a lawful pursuit. The suspect was eventually caught, prosecuted and convicted and is off the streets for a long time. All this is very good police work that more than deserves to be rewarded. The question is, what type of reward? The question also is, what can you do as a sergeant?

The Police Assessment Center: Important Keys for Success

If your department allows it, maybe you could tell your assessors that you will write up a commendation to place in the pursuing officer's personnel file. If not, you could tell your assessors that you will make a recommendation of commendation to whomever in the chain of command can prepare the commendation. Be as **specific** here as possible. For example: you could tell the assessors that you verbally commended the officer for his **excellent observation in locating a wanted felon**. However since only your lieutenant can commend the officer on paper, you tell the assessors that you will prepare a report to the lieutenant on the officer's good work, with your recommendation that the lieutenant write up a formal commendation. Alternately, you can be more creative and tell the assessors that you will write up the commendation for the lieutenant's signature.

On the other hand, in this scenario the same officer ran a red light and caused a serious accident. The officer obviously did not want to have this accident, but his violation of the traffic regulations made it his fault, no matter how much emergency equipment he had activated. Exactly as you had to do for the reward part of this scenario, you must know your department's boundaries and rules of discipline. And exactly as you did in the preceding example, you must tell your assessors what you are going to do or what you are going to recommend to be done by the appropriate rank. And again, **be specific.** I can't stress this enough.

For example: you could tell the assessors that you can't impose discipline but you are going to recommend to the lieutenant that the officer be cited for failure to slow down at a controlled intersection. You could also tell the lieutenant that because of the serious injuries caused by the officer's carelessness, you recommend the maximum allowed penalty, a five-day suspension. This is not at all to say that you have to show the assessors that you are unreasonably tough. If the allowable suspension for an offense of this nature is one to five days, you could recommend anything from two to five, depending on the officer's history. Here again, you can be creative: you can tell the assessors that you will look into the officer's traffic record. If you find that he has not been disciplined for any flagrant traffic violations, you will recommend that he serve only a one-day suspension, with four days held in abeyance. If the officer commits another flagrant or similar offense within a three-year period, he has to serve the other four days that were held in abeyance, in addition to his punishment for the second offense.

In the above punishment scenario, I recommended creativity only because the officer was instrumental in taking a violent felon off the streets. Make sure to tell the assessors that. Being creative like this will usually make your assessors smile, at least inside, and that can't ever hurt you; it will only help you.

Again, know what you can and can't do. In addition, know what the other ranks can and can't do. Know the ranges for reward and discipline. There is usually no "right way" of doing things regarding reward and discipline.

The Police Assessment Center: Important Keys for Success

You can also use **training** as a very effective follow-up in all situations. This will work to your advantage; most candidates in their nervousness and anxiety forget about this valuable tool. In the aforementioned scenario, you might tell your assessors that you will conduct roll-call training on officer responsibilities regarding traffic regulations in vehicular pursuits. You might also tell the assessors you will personally conduct training on when the officers can and can't initiate pursuits. You could have the officer who crashed take a remedial driver training course. All of these things are training tools you can use very effectively as your follow-up. Again, **and I emphasize,** even if you personally can't do these things at your rank of sergeant, make sure you know who can, and tell the assessors that you will recommend they be done by the appropriate person.

We have spent a lot of time on follow-up on issues with your personnel; now let's talk about follow-up with the actual scenario. The previous chapter's hostage situation scenario, regardless of how it played out, should become an important roll-call topic of discussion. You should tell the assessors that during roll call you will discuss both the things done well and not so well. Further, you should encourage input and suggestions for improvement from the rank and file. Regardless of how well everyone performed in the scenario, believe me, there is always room for improvement. For example, tell the assessors that SWAT team members will be invited to attend roll calls to answer any questions, to explain why they do the things they do and to respond to any praise or criticism. Tell the assessors that you will spend roll calls going over the department's specific written directives or general orders as they pertain to hostage situations. **Emphasize your use of roll calls** so that all the officers on all shifts and with different days off will benefit from this review.

Regarding any action scenario that you might receive, including the previous hostage one, formal written follow-up is critical. If an after-action report is required, **you** do it. If it's not required, do it anyway. Again, to get the extra credit, it is not good enough to tell the assessors that you will prepare the report. Think baby steps. Instead, tell the assessors that you will prepare the report for a specific police official's information, then list how you will route it, depending on your specific department's protocol. For example: to the district commander, through the sector captain, through the section lieutenant. You tell the assessors exactly how you will format the report and what you will include in the report. For example again: you will prepare a brief synopsis or overview, then a detailed and specific report of the incident. You will include in the report the things that worked and the things that did not. The last part of the report will be your recommendations regarding improvements or corrections that need to be made in the future for the specific type of scenario that you had. Conversely, if certain things worked very well, you would recommend that they be incorporated into future departmental standard operating procedures.

The Police Assessment Center: Important Keys for Success

Then you do the things that you can do immediately, before the report goes through channels and spends several weeks or months being reviewed and re-reviewed. Let's take the hostage situation again. Again depending on what rank you are competing for (remember, **even if you at your rank can't do it, you can always recommend that the person at the appropriate rank can**), you can do the following:

Immediately provide the major community leaders in the surrounding areas with enough facts about the situation to give them a basic understanding of what transpired. Here again, be as specific as possible by telling your assessors **who** you will notify, **what** you will tell them, **why** you will do so and **how** you will go about it. For example:

WHO

a. You notify the area block captains, the neighborhood watch leaders and the area neighborhood council leader.

WHAT

b. You tell these community leaders that a domestic dispute involving the custody of a baby resulted in the ex-husband's arrest without incident and that the baby is OK. Tell the assessors that you will avoid giving the leaders much more information now, because it probably would interfere with the successful prosecution of the case. Upon a final resolution, you make it clear you will be glad to meet with them to answer more questions about the details of the incident.

WHY

c. Tell the assessors that you are notifying the community leaders in order to eliminate any fear of what they might typically infer—that *they* might become a victim of this same type of crime. Telling them the truth in this case—that this was an isolated incident—is an important step in reducing the community's fear of crime. It will stop in its tracks any unnecessary fear that inevitably and understandably occurs after such an incident.

HOW

d. Tell the assessors that you will notify these community leaders *in person* if at all possible. A hands-on approach will foster greater respect for your message among the leaders and allows for direct feedback. This is far preferable to phone calls, which are much less personal, or e-mails, which can be lost or delayed in cyberspace or misinterpreted or misunderstood.

e. State that you will convene a community meeting as soon as possible. This meeting will be held no more than three or four days after the incident—again, the sooner the better. You will prepare a written notice of this meeting, which will be in flyer form and will briefly summarize the purpose of the meeting, in this case to inform citizens about the incident. The flyer will contain the **location, time and date** of the meeting and will be printed immediately, within no more than one or two days after the incident.

f. Tell the assessors you will hand deliver copies of this flyer to the community leaders. If, because of the short notice, you are unable to meet them personally, you will arrange for one of your patrol units to do so in your place.

g. You will make arrangements to have at the meeting any police officials who can answer any questions you cannot or whose presence simply lends credibility to the way the situation was resolved. For example, you would have in attendance the SWAT team official in charge of the entry response team into the house. This official could address the citizens' concerns about specific tactics the SWAT team employed to take the prisoner into custody.

h. You will prepare a brief written agenda before the meeting to pass out to the citizens when they arrive. The agenda should never be more than one page; a half-page is preferable. The agenda should list the hostage situation as the main topic. Some other issues can be listed in the agenda but should not be major ones at this particular meeting. The citizens will be focused on this one hostage situation, and when all the issues surrounding it are at least temporarily resolved, they will probably lose interest in the meeting and just want to leave.

i. At the meeting, you will ensure the presence of as many officers as possible who regularly patrol the specific area of the hostage incident. This is to ensure that before and after the meeting citizens can actually see the faces of those responsible for their safety and who can specifically address their concerns.

In all honesty, I could go on and on with this one. Taking these follow-up steps will put you ahead of most of your peers in this type of exercise. In a real life situation, these are the right things to do; they will make it much easier for you to foster positive relationships within the community, especially following serious criminal incidents.

Important Point to Remember

- Constantly think about issues, actions and follow-up actions when addressing and handling each assessment center exercise.

- These three critical points are listed in their order of importance to your assessors in evaluating you.

- You *must* make sure you demonstrate to your assessors that you know the issues. However obvious the issues may seem to you, make sure you express them to the assessors.

- When taking actions and follow-up actions, you can never be too specific. Consider even overdoing attention to detail.

- Whenever possible, be as creative as you can, especially when taking actions.

- You can never overemphasize the importance of training. Employ training as often as possible in your follow-up actions.

Chapter 8

THE RELEVANCE OF DELEGATION

At first it might seem odd to dedicate an entire chapter to the concept of delegation. For the purpose of this discussion, delegation will simply mean **assigning to someone else a task that was originally given to you**, whether the task is performed in the field or administratively. Bear with me, though, as this is another important concept that needs some explanation based on the past and the evolving nature of police department assessment testing and actual police department employees. Let me first say that I am not one who believes that, in general, the way things were done in the past was necessarily better than the way they are done today. Not only is that not true, there could be volumes written about the many things that police departments do better today than they used to.

Secondly, what I am going to say regarding delegation has never been and probably will never be proven statistically or factually. In small part, it is based on my two and a half years as a test development specialist for my department; mostly, though, it is based on what I saw in my thirty-three and a half years as a police officer. It is also based on almost as much time spent in joint and collaborative police work experience with other departments, both locally and nationwide. And it is based on my experience in *all of the ranks that I have held*, dealing personally with members of my and other departments at all ranks up to and including chief of police. It is based somewhat on numerous candid, mostly one-on-one conversations with officers and officials on these departments. Finally, it is based on an admittedly limited but very recent knowledge of and personal participation in other departments' assessment centers, and my involvement in the development of my own department's assessment center.

Now, please do not take this personally, but for whatever reason, the fact is that today's police officials perform at a recognizably significant lower level, both in the field and administratively, than those of twenty or thirty years ago.

Whether or not you take this personally, or whether or not you believe it to be true, let's see how you can apply this statement to what you do and how it translates into your performance at your department's assessment center.

Twenty and thirty years ago, most police department assessment centers were conceptually very different than what they are today. First of all, the administrative part of the testing was created so

The Police Assessment Center: Important Keys for Success

that only an exceptional candidate could complete the exercise in its entirety in the allotted time. The reason for this was to test the candidate's ability to prioritize the administrative tasks. In other words, the assessment centers wanted the candidates to separate the tasks, from most important to least important, and then complete the most important ones as best they could. For the remainder of the items, they expected the candidates to delegate the tasks to other officers or officials as appropriate. For example, the exercise might be to see how a lieutenant handled his or her in-basket, which contained the following items:

1. A letter from a citizens' group complaining of noise in the neighborhood.

2. A use-of-taser report involving an injured suspect charged with assault on a police officer. The report contains numerous witness statements requiring an investigative write-up. The investigation, with recommendations, is due that day.

3. A list of community meetings requiring attendance. Two of the meetings are on the same day at the same time, and one of the meetings is on the lieutenant's day off.

4. A letter from an officer's wife complaining that she thinks her husband is having an affair with another woman.

5. A note from a sergeant requesting a meeting with the lieutenant. The female sergeant feels that the male sergeants are not pulling

their load and that she is being singled out, because of her gender, to pick up their slack.

6. A letter from a citizen complaining of a parking ticket he received at 4 a.m. on a Sunday morning because his vehicle's wheels were too far from the curb.

7. A memorandum from a captain to prepare an action plan to combat auto thefts in a specific neighborhood. The memorandum is due that day.

For the purposes of simplicity and ease of explanation and understanding, this example in-basket contains only seven items. We'll make the time limit one hour for this mock exercise. In reality, you could have any number of items to handle. Most of the in-basket exercises that I have seen or personally helped create were made up of from ten to twenty specific items, and the candidate had from between one and a half to three hours to complete them.

In the past, the candidate would first have been expected to **link** any items where appropriate. While there will be no chapter on the concept of linkage, I must digress a bit here and discuss it briefly, as it still is important today, just not as much as in the past. Very simply, the candidate would have been expected to link or join together any items that were related in terms of geographical location, time of occurrence, method of operation, suspect description and so on.

The Police Assessment Center: Important Keys for Success

Secondly, in the past, the candidate was expected to separate the **priority items** from the non-priority ones. For example, let's say that the scenario you are given indicates that the suspect in item 2 was initially stopped because he was acting suspiciously, looking into several automobiles. He then became combative, had to be forcefully subdued using a taser, and was subsequently charged with assault on a police officer. The neighborhood referred to in item 7 was the same neighborhood in which the suspect in item 2 was arrested. The candidate would then have been expected to join items 2 and 7 together, or link them. Specifically, the candidate would have done the investigative write-up and prepared an action plan for the captain. But as part of the action plan, the candidate would have actually demonstrated how, in fact, the items could be linked.

The action plan could contain some type of manpower redeployment based on the times of day and the days of the week of the auto thefts. It might create a special tactical unit, such as a uniformed or nonuniformed bicycle patrol. Then, to actually demonstrate to your assessors that you really understood *how* items 2 and 7 could be linked, you would tell the assessors that since the suspect in item 2 was in the same neighborhood as the one for which you are preparing an action plan in item 7 to fight auto thefts, you would assign a detective to handle the investigation. The detective would be specifically assigned to debrief the suspect.

Thirdly, you recognized that your priority items were numbers 2 and 7. It is common sense that these two items are priorities, plus you were given a specific due date for their completion. That's basically all you would have to do for items 2 and 7. You identified the two priority items, which happened to be linked, and took action on them that day. You prepared the action plan and made sure that the detective debriefed the suspect in #2, who might have been linked to the problem in #7.

Today, things are a bit different. For practical purposes in the field, you would ensure that a detective conducted the investigation, but for assessment center purposes, the assessors wants you to demonstrate that *you* know exactly what the detective needs to do for a successful investigation. Again, even though in reality you would delegate to a detective, you must demonstrate that you know the basics of what the detective must do.

To get that little extra during the assessment, *you personally* would make sure that the suspect in item 2 is interviewed or debriefed by a detective, after ensuring he is read his Miranda rights. You personally would follow up with the specific appropriate detective as to whether the suspect had knowledge of who committed the automobile thefts or if the suspect confessed to the crimes himself. By appropriate detective, I mean don't assign a crime-against-persons detective to the case if a crime-against-property detective should handle it. Give the assessors a specific detective's name if possible. You would—for this exercise and unless told otherwise—assume that the suspect does not admit to the other thefts. You would make sure the detective shows any witnesses to any of the auto thefts a photo spread to possibly identify the suspect. If that fails, you would make sure the detective follows up with a lineup.

This may be an oversimplified example, but it demonstrates the fact that even when it is truly appropriate for you to delegate a task, you are **demonstrating to the assessors that you know** what needs to be done, **can do it yourself**, and therefore are at the top of your game to supervise and/or manage the investigative process effectively. You have gone above and beyond simply assigning the case or making sure the case is assigned to a detective or investigator.

In demonstrating all of the above to your assessors, you are performing what we sometimes refer to as taking baby steps. You should think of these baby steps as attention to the simplest of details. Think of these steps as if you were teaching new students the very basics of what to do in these situations.

To close on this theme of baby steps, let me use the non-police-related demonstration I have used in each of my assessment center preparation classes. Your immediate supervisor gives you the task of emptying the trash at the end of the day, today, but tells you that you yourself cannot perform the task. You must make sure that it is done, however. Your failure to have this task properly performed will result in your losing your nice government job, retirement pension, and probably your house and significant other. How do you accomplish this task? The answer is simple. You use baby steps. They are as follows:

1. Assign one specific person to the task.

2. Assign another specific person as a backup in case the first specific person comes down with a last-minute catastrophic illness and can't take out the trash.

3. Make sure that the person assigned to the task has numerous functioning means to contact you in case he or she is disabled. This includes telephone, pager, emergency wallet notification card, etc.

4. Call both persons into your office and show them the containers for recycled trash and regular trash.

5. Explain to each that the trash bags must be lifted from the cans and then securely tied at the tops with bag-ties. At that time, show them both where the fresh bags and bag-ties are located.

6. Further explain that the bags are then to be taken out to the dumpsters and deposited in the particular dumpster corresponding to the recyclables and the regular trash.

7. Then physically show both people exactly where the specific dumpsters are.

8. Upon completing the task, tell them that they are to report back to your office, get new trash bags, and place them into the trash containers.

The Police Assessment Center: Important Keys for Success

9. Tell both people that they are to report back to you that the trash was successfully deposited in the Dumpsters. If you are not available, as you may be called away from your office, they are to leave you a written note documenting that they completed the task. (You could have told them to call you on your cell phone, but leaving written documentation is better, as you might not be able to answer your phone, don't have it with you, etc.)

10. Give both people a hard-copy piece of paper with the above instructions clearly written out, and have them both explain to you what their task is. Ask them if they have any questions, and if they do, answer them at that time.

11. As soon as physically possible, personally check your trash cans to make sure they are empty. If they are, as soon as practically possible, personally notify the supervisor who gave you the trash assignment that it was successfully handled. If you are unable to do this in person, notify the supervisor by phone or leave a written note on the supervisor's desk. E-mails are fine as alternatives, but they have a better chance of getting lost or not being received in a timely manner than personal notifications or hard-copy written notes.

By doing all of the above, you are making sure the task will be performed. You have taken the task of taking out the trash and broken it down into the most basic of steps—baby steps. You demonstrated your specific knowledge of the task itself, explained it specifically to your subordinates, made sure they understood it themselves, and then received follow-up documentation that the task had been completed. You then made follow-up notification to your supervisor that the job was completed properly.

You need to remember this example. You were told to delegate this task. Most competitors at an assessment center would simply have assigned an appropriate person who was working at the time, made sure that the person was notified properly and in a timely fashion, and perhaps checked to see that the assignment was completed. You did so much more. You made all human attempts within reason to ensure that the job was not only done but done properly. By taking all of those baby steps, you told the assessors not only that you could direct and manage the task, but that you knew the exact details of what the job entailed. This attention to detail will definitely get you a step up on your competition. Not only that, you will be able to apply this example, in countless ways, to practical on-the-street and administrative situations.

In closing this chapter, I want to share with you the abbreviated but very true example of what doing it yourself versus delegating meant to a fellow career police officer whom I personally worked with. I am going to change some details of the assessment center exercise given to my peer and associate, but the general facts are accurate.

The Police Assessment Center: Important Keys for Success

There was an opening for a chief-of-police job in a small but upscale resort city. The city was occupied by mostly conservative, middle-class people of all ethnicities. There was, however, a rapid influx of very rich, liberal, anti-war activists who were, many thought, trying to take over the city. They were buying most of the available homes for personal residences, as well as almost all of the available retail space, setting up some alternative-lifestyle businesses that were on the questionable side to the overall conservative population. Because these people had so much money, there was really nothing the majority population could do to stop them.

The city encouraged applications from all over the country. Because it was a beautiful but small resort city with a very low crime rate and an attractive pay package, the vacancy announcement attracted numerous qualified applicants from all over the country. Most of the applicants included high-ranking officials and chiefs of police from state and municipal police forces. My fellow officer and peer, who applied, was not a high-ranking official, but like me, a lieutenant, which in our department was considered a lower-level manager. He had just completed his twenty years of service so he could retire and receive a pension. He wanted to remain in law enforcement, however, and felt he could be a good police chief in the right environment.

After submitting written applications, he and the other applicants went through an interview process. Through the interview process, certain applicants were chosen as finalists who then had to compete in an assessment center exercise.

After several weeks, I received a visit at my police district from a retired, very high-ranking state police official from a large Eastern state. He identified himself as the person in charge of the assessment center for this chief-of-police selection process. He wanted to interview me, as my fellow police lieutenant had given him my name as a reference.

The interview was very brief and to the point. The questions he asked me were, as best as I can remember, mostly about character and work ethic issues. The interview lasted only about ten minutes. Because I was surprised at the brevity and nonspecificity of the interview, I asked him if there was even a chance that my fellow official was still in the running for the job. The official's response was, "He's already got it."

Boy, was I surprised. I then asked if he would not mind telling me just a little bit about how and why my fellow lieutenant had done so well. The first thing he said was, "Barry, it was not even close. He blew everyone away at the assessment center." I then asked him to please give me an example of a scenario or exercise in which he had performed so much better than everyone else. The following is the short version of one of those scenarios. For the purposes of confidentiality and anonymity, I have changed some information.

The Police Assessment Center: Important Keys for Success

Scenario: You have just been sworn in as the chief of police. You must work the day-work tour of duty. Your days off are Sunday and Saturday, and cannot change without approval of the mayor. The month is May. The liberal anti-war activists are moving into the city in droves. They have just obtained permits to have a parade on the boardwalk every Saturday afternoon, all summer long, from Memorial Day until Labor Day. The same group has also obtained permits to have a large area of the beach reserved for picnicking, for their use only, every Sunday afternoon, also for the entire summer.

(Each candidate was then given a deployment sheet and a roster, detailing who the regular and special summer season officers and officials were, their assignments, tours of duty and days off. I was never told nor did I ask for specifics on this manpower, but I know personally that because it was a very prosperous and well-maintained city, they had or could acquire at least adequate police resources to maintain good order during the busy summer months.)

The mayor does not expect any serious problems with these functions on the beach and boardwalk. He does anticipate, though, that the influx of these people and their taking over certain areas of the beach and boardwalk, for extended periods of time all summer, will create some opposition and animosity among many of the conservative, long-time residents. He wants to avoid, if at all possible, any open confrontations between new and long-time residents. The mayor wants you to give him a breakdown of how you will deploy the members of your department to best ensure this goal.

The official told me that all of the candidates deployed various officers and officials in differing amounts during the two critical times, the parade on Saturday and the picnic on Sunday, all summer long. Some set up special details, some changed officers' days off, some changed officers' tours, etc.

Response that blew everyone away: My peer (who incidentally turned out to be the lowest-ranking candidate in the assessment center for the chief position), did all of the above but included the following: *He told the assessors that he would personally work and be in charge of the detail every Saturday and Sunday.* The assessors then told him that he had to take Saturdays and Sundays as his days off. He told them that because of the importance of keeping order during these brand-new events, he would personally ensure that they went off without problems by working himself. When the assessors told him that by doing so he would have to work all summer, without a day off, his reply was, "That's fine with me, at least during my first year on the job."

I don't know if after becoming chief he actually did what he said, but knowing him personally, I will bet if there were special events or activities that did have the potential for serious order-maintenance issues, he was there, in charge. I think he served as chief there for about seven years or so, eventually becoming the victim of political differences with those in charge of the city, and moved on to a different area of law enforcement. Some of you will say that he definitely micromanaged, and should have delegated authority unless the officials delegated to manage the Friday and Saturday events were unable to handle them successfully. Personally, I agree. I don't think it is necessary for a new chief of police not to have a day off all summer. Further, it's unhealthy, both physically and mentally.

This is an extreme example of doing things yourself, but his answer worked beautifully. I'm definitely not saying to be dishonest to your assessors by telling them you would do things that you actually would not do in a real situation. I am, however, telling you that you sometimes will get only one shot in life at something you really want. To set yourself apart from the others who are also playing the assessment game, go extra miles on a big-time basis. Always remember that when you go those extra miles and do the managing yourself and don't take any days off, make sure you tell your assessors why. In this example you would tell them the following:

1. You have to be there, as you are new and are learning everything you can about these new groups of citizens who might possibly conflict with older, established residents.

2. You will be hands-on your first year, and if all goes well during the first summer, next summer you will consider delegating the management of these activities.

3. By personally managing these events, you will get to know other officials working the events with you. This will enable you to see who is qualified and able to assist you next year in taking the lead or in assisting at these events.

4. The mayor is holding you personally responsible for maintaining good order during these events. If people you delegate to blow it during your first summer, you are probably not going to get another chance. There went your dream, because you will be fired.

Most of you will not become chiefs of police, nor do most of you aspire to. Please, though, remember this scenario. You can apply the simple concepts in the handling of it in your steps up the promotional ladder.

The Police Assessment Center: Important Keys for Success

Important Points to Remember

- Your ability to delegate a task or responsibility is probably not one of the key concepts your assessment center is measuring. I say probably because there is always the possibility that some department's chief somewhere in the country will decide that this is what he or she deems important.

- Unless the above applies, and it is incredibly unlikely that it will, delegate as little as possible.

- Your department is evaluating how you perform the task, do the job and take the responsibility, not how well you can delegate.

- Even when delegation is appropriate, tell the assessors much more. Demonstrate that you know how to perform the task. Do this by telling the person to whom you are delegating the specifics of what he or she must do. Then make sure that he completed the assignment using follow-up.

Chapter 9

SIMPLE KEYS TO ASSESSMENT CENTER SUCCESS

In this last chapter I am going to ramble a little bit. I will present you with some final thoughts and points, in no particular order, that are extremely important not only to your success at the assessment center but also later in your field activities. They originate from mistakes that I have made in my career and from areas in which I have personally come up short.

Due Dates

If you are given a due date on an assignment, make sure you complete it on that day. If the assignment involves a situation for which you need to do more work—such as interviewing witnesses who may be out of town, interviewing officers who are on leave, contacting government agencies on weekends, etc.—still complete it as best you can on that day. Do, though, let your assessors know that you will make every reasonable **attempt** to go out of town **that day** to interview witnesses, to call in the officers **that day** who are on leave, to utilize any existing weekend or emergency notification services to contact the necessary government agencies **that day,** etc. Finally, let the assessors know that if the above means are fruitless, you will request an extension (**and be date specific**) from the official giving you the assignment.

Meetings

Always attend meetings that you are assigned. No exceptions. Here's how you do it. Let's say your exercise involves you working the day-work tour of duty, 0800 to 1600 hours. You are assigned four meetings that day. There's a neighborhood watch meeting at 1300, a boys and girls club meeting at 1300, a business association meeting at 1300, and a youth roving patrol meeting at 1900 hours. First, you assign three specific officers or officials to represent you at each of the 1300-hours meetings. (Make sure you give the assessors the names of the officers/officials, ensuring that they are working and not on leave or days off). You brief the officers/officials thoroughly on issues that need to be addressed or problems that might be brought up at the meetings. They are **your representatives** who will attend the meetings. You then make sure that you also **personally**

The Police Assessment Center: Important Keys for Success

attend each of the meetings. At each meeting, you explain that you can stay only briefly, as you have two others to attend. You explain that your representatives will provide you feedback and that you will personally meet with leaders of the meeting or any other members at their convenience should there be matters that the officers or officials in your place could not handle. Finally, you tell the members that you will do whatever it takes so that in the future, these meetings will either be staggered better on the same day or held on different days.

Now, how about the 1900 hours meeting? Your day has not been much fun, and neither will your evening, for you will notify your assessors that you will personally attend the 1900 hours meeting. You will remain there for the entire meeting, with no representative to allow you to leave a little early. Then, before you leave work, you prepare a short memorandum or note to the official assigning you these meetings that you would like to meet with him as soon as possible to discuss new scheduling so that you can attend each day-work meeting in its entirety. As for the 1900 hours meeting when you are on day-work, you suck it up. That's part of being a police official. It's not very different from when you were an officer and had a late arrest with lots of witnesses to interview and a carload of property to recover. The only difference is that, when you were an officer, you were probably compensated with compensatory time or overtime; now that you are a supervisor or manager, you may not be, depending on your department's personnel regulations.

Barry T. Malkin

Community Policing

Make sure you thoroughly understand the concept of **community policing**. Chances are, you will be given a problem at your assessment center that will involve some, if not all of the principles of community policing. If you have to, go to a police library or find as many resources as you can on this topic. It is not only not a difficult concept to understand, it is the basic **problem-solving** many of us old-timers did when we walked the old-fashioned **police beats** you sometimes see in movies of the fifties and sixties. We did not use the term "community policing," we simply referred to the concept as "cultivating your beat." Let me give you a brief, very simple example of how a single beat cop, walking an assigned foot-beat in a community, community policed. You can apply this example to any crime or order maintenance problem you may be given.

Officer Walker is working the day-work tour of duty. She talks to various neighbors and businesspeople who complain of broken business and car windows in the area. She knows that this is a problem because frequently upon arrival at work in the morning, she has to make reports of these incidents. Clearly now, she has **identified the problem.**

Officer Walker now tries to get a clear **understanding of the problem.** She talks to the neighbors and businesspeople, who tell her that the windows are broken by kids playing baseball in the streets after school, after she checks off duty. Officer Walker investigates further by

The Police Assessment Center: Important Keys for Success

checking with the crime analysis unit to get a possible **specific history of the problem**. This is very important. (I say "specific" because you want your assessors to know that it's the very recent past that's important, not what happened two or three years ago.) She checks back six months later and finds that in all of the broken window incident reports, there was no vandalism or property stolen. She also finds that in some of the broken window reports, kids did admit that they broke the windows accidentally and were responsible. They also said that they played ball in the streets because the old field that they used to play on was not only filled with trash and broken bottles, but frequently occupied by drunks and drug dealers. In fact, the kids had named the field "thug and drug park."

Officer Walker now **creates a plan of action** to solve the problem. Remember, you are not going to get full cooperation or even any cooperation in some of these actions you take in your assessment center, but you perform for your assessors as if you are in a perfect world. She needs to have the field cleaned up so the kids can play on it. She will need to have short-term operations to make undercover observations, then drug buys and busts. She will then need to meet with school administrators to develop the best ways to encourage the kids to play on the field after the crime and maintenance problems are alleviated.

Officer Walker now **takes action** to fully implement her plan. She presents the plan to her officials. She requests from her officials that she be placed on the evening tour of duty to implement the plan. The reason for the evening tour is that she can both notify all of the involved parties and agencies, and also be there to monitor and be directly involved in the various operations and activities. She then notifies the **vice unit** to do the buy busts. She notifies the **city agency** responsible to clean up the park. She works with school administrators to hold an assembly in which she can explain to the kids what is being done to clean up the park, and why it is now safe to play there.

Again, for assessment center purposes, we assume Officer Walker was successful in providing a place for kids to play ball after school. To involve the community and encourage and enable the continued success of her efforts, she creates an activity to bring everyone involved together. She has a cookout in the field. She asks merchants and business leaders for donations of hamburgers and hotdogs, borrows a grill or two from someone, finds a boom box for some tunes, and if she's lucky gets some neighborhood kids to get a band together and perform. She makes sure that she invites the members of the city agency who cleaned up the field as well as some of the vice officers who made the "buy-busts." She also invites the entire community and makes a point at the cookout, when she has them all together in a festive mood, to try to buy them into becoming part of a permanent volunteer program to maintain the viability of the park. Officer Walker is **rewarding** her team and **celebrating** their successful operation with the cookout; then they are assisting her in maintaining successful **follow-up** with neighborhood volunteers.

The Police Assessment Center: Important Keys for Success

Some Final Thoughts

Think **notifications** as you participate in your assessment center. Think of that word constantly. When you are preparing any sort of crime or order maintenance action plan, notify as many city, state or county agencies outside of your own who can and should be involved, to assist you. When you complete your plan or operation, notify those in the police chain of command both above and below of its success. (Again, always assume you are achieving success while addressing the assessment center issues.) Notify all of the members of the business and citizen associations in person, if at all possible, by **attending their meetings** or **holding meetings of your own**. The majority of the community will not be able to be notified in this way, so notify them by preparing flyers and personally leaving them at their residences, or telephoning them or sending e-mails as appropriate.

Upon receipt of any written correspondence or telephone message from a citizen or business concerning a complaint or even a commendation, immediately personally notify the citizen or business that you received the correspondence or message. This is very important in real-time police work and is often overlooked by assessment center candidates. First, it validates that the correspondence from the citizen or business is of concern to you. Second, you are demonstrating to the assessors that you successfully completed the "policing 101" second-day lesson, making sure that the correspondence or telephone call you received **was in fact** sent or made by the person or business representing itself.

Whether your assessment center scenarios must be handled orally or in writing as part of an in-basket exercise, all of the concepts in this book apply in the same way. Just remember, if you are handling your exercises in writing or on a computer, the assessors can't question you. They have only one way of knowing what you are thinking: by your responses. Err on the side of writing too much, especially in dealing with your recognition of key issues and follow-up actions.

On a personal note, the very first day I assumed command of the Georgetown Sector of Washington, DC, my commander, now the late Inspector Kenneth Hutson, who also happened to be my personal friend, called me into his office. He shook my hand, hugged me, congratulated me on my promotion and asked me to sit down. After briefing me on my new assignment, he ended the conversation with these exact words: "I know that you are going to be a great captain. There are only two things, though, that will make you an outstanding one. No matter what, each day when you come in to work, take your phone messages from the previous evening, and return all of your telephone calls immediately. Next, no matter what, personally attend all of your community and business meetings. That's it, and good luck."

Finally, good luck to each and every one of you. Remember, this assessment center is maybe your **one shot** at changing and/or improving your career path and lifestyle. Take chances, and be as creative as possible. Your assessors will not knock you down for doing so; it can

The Police Assessment Center: Important Keys for Success

only grab their attention at the very least, and will probably boost you up past many of your competitors.

It took me the better part of twenty-three years to learn and to use the points that I have presented to you in this book, while competing in my own assessment centers. Hopefully, this book will make this process a lot easier for you.

Important Points to Remember

- Strictly comply with the due dates you are given. If you are assigning a task to anyone, without exception always assign a due date for completion.

- Always attend your meetings and return your phone calls. No matter how creative you have to be, attend all of your meetings for at least a few minutes.

- Especially if you cannot attend the entire meeting due to conflicts, arrange for specific follow-up. Have your representative meet with you after the meeting to inform you of any issues needing action. Then take the action, notify the appropriate individuals and agencies, set up a follow-up meeting, etc.

- When competing in your assessment center, constantly think about notifications. Your assessors don't know if you know things unless you tell them in person or in writing. They can't read your mind. You must notify them.

- When appropriate in specific exercises, notify both those below and those above you in rank of the actions you take. Also when appropriate in these exercises, notify as many applicable local and federal agencies as possible of the issues you have and actions and/or follow-up actions you take.

- Make sure you thoroughly understand the concept of community policing. Be creative in implementing it when you feel it's appropriate. It will never hurt and can only help you.